London A to Z

Stephen Brock
Anne Vaughan

Cornelsen

London A to Z

Im Auftrage des Verlages erarbeitet von
Stephen Brock und Anne Vaughan

Beratende Mitwirkung und Übungen zu den Texten
Prof. Dr. Liesel Hermes, Karlsruhe

Bildquellen
s. Verzeichnis auf S. 37

1. Auflage ✓ €   Druck 9 8 7 6 Jahr 03 02 01 2000
Alle Drucke dieser Auflage können im Unterricht nebeneinander verwendet werden.

Druck: Druck-Centrum Fürst, Berlin

ISBN 3-464-05852-2

Bestellnummer 58522

gedruckt auf säurefreiem Papier, umweltschonend hergestellt aus chlorfrei gebleichten Faserstoffen

Contents

AIRPORT TO NEW CROSS

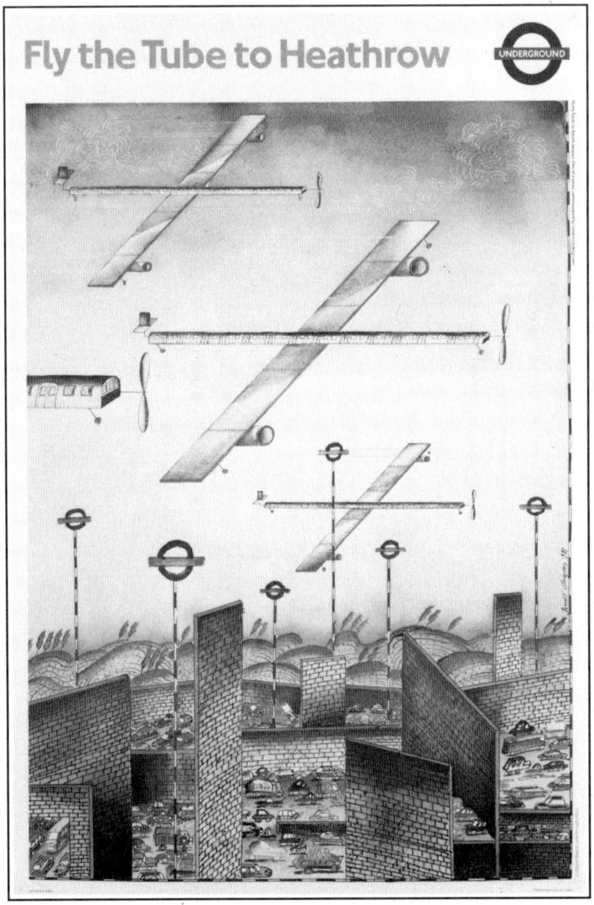

"The weather in London is warm and sunny. The time is 9 am. Thank you for flying with Eastern Airlines. Have a nice day." The steward smiled and sat down*. The Patterson family could* see Heathrow Airport under them. Then their jumbo jet from New York landed in London. Everybody went into the terminal building*.

"Where's Aunt Jenny?" asked Don Patterson. "Why isn't she here?"
"We need a telephone," said Mr Patterson. "Perhaps Aunt Jenny couldn't come."
"There's a phone," said Cindy, Don's sister, and pointed to a yellow phone box. A few minutes later, Mr Patterson returned.
"Aunt Jenny's car has broken down*," he said. "We've got to find our way to New Cross alone."
"Where's New Cross?" asked Cindy.
"In south-east* London," said Mrs Patterson.
"How do we get there?" asked Don.
"By tube*. That's the underground railway*," said Mrs Patterson. "The station is in the airport. Here it is." Mr Patterson bought four tickets at the ticket office.
"Does the train go to New Cross?" Mr Patterson asked.
"You've got to change at South Kensington and Whitechapel," the man said. "It's a long way, you know. The airport is fifteen miles west* of the centre of London."

The train came and the Pattersons got on. Forty minutes later they changed trains at South Kensington. The second train was very full. They got off at Whitechapel and changed again for New Cross. Everybody was really tired now.

Aunt Jenny was waiting at New Cross station.
"What a journey! Thirty-four stations – it took almost two hours!" said Don.
"Oh, that isn't bad," said Aunt Jenny. "The journey takes an hour and a half by car!" There was a poster on the platform. It said,

sat down = *setzte sich hin;* could = *konnte;* terminal building = *Flughafengebäude;* has broken down = *hat eine Panne;* south-east = *Südost;* tube = *U-Bahn;* railway = *Eisenbahn;* west = *westlich*

Battersea Christmas Dogs

"Boring, boring, boring! I always look forward to Christmas* for weeks and weeks. On Christmas morning I open my presents and then I'm bored." Kerry put her presents on her bed. There was a good TV programme on at three o'clock - an adventure film. But it was still only ten o'clock in the morning. Her parents were busy in the kitchen* and lunch was always at one o'clock on Christmas Day.

"I know!" she thought. "I'll take Angus for a walk." Angus was the family's dog, an old white Scottish terrier. "Angus! Walkies!" she called. "Mum, Dad!" Kerry called into the kitchen. "I'm taking Angus to the Common* for a walk. OK?"
"Yes, good idea, Kerry," said Mrs Martin. "But don't be late home."
"OK. Bye!" Kerry got the dog's ball and left the house with Angus.

The Martins' house wasn't far from Tooting Bec Common, a big park in South London. Kerry liked Tooting Bec Common. There was a small lake with lots of birds on it. Angus liked the park, too. He could meet the other dogs there and run races with them. Angus ran to the nearest dog and barked*. But the dog didn't want to play with him.

Kerry threw* the ball and Angus fetched it. He enjoyed this game. "He can play this game all day," thought Kerry. She was bored with Angus. "But I can't." She threw the ball hard and it flew into some trees*. Angus barked and ran after it. Kerry walked and watched the birds on the lake for a long time. "Where's Angus?" she thought. She went to the trees and found the ball, but Angus wasn't there. "Angus! Come here, boy!" she called, but no white dog came. "Silly old animal," she thought. She called and called, but Angus didn't come. She looked at her watch. It was quarter to one – almost time for lunch. "Oh, well," she thought. "Perhaps he has gone home alone." So she went back home. At five minutes to one, Kerry opened the door.

"Is that you, Kerry?" called Mrs Martin from the kitchen.
"Yes, is Angus here?" asked Kerry.
"No," said Mr Martin. "Didn't he come home with you?"
"He ran into some trees and didn't come back. I don't know where he is," answered Kerry.
"Don't worry. Let's have our lunch quickly. Then we can go and look for him," said her father.
"Oh, Dad, have I got to go with you? I want to watch that film on TV this afternoon!" said Kerry.
"You can watch TV when we've found the dog," said Mrs Martin.
After lunch, Kerry and her parents went to Tooting Bec Common, but they couldn't find the dog. Angus didn't come home that day or that night. Everybody was very worried.

Next morning, Mr Martin said, "I'm going to Battersea Dogs Home."
"Do you think Angus is there?" asked Kerry.

"Perhaps," answered her father. "They've got hundreds of animals."
"I'll come with you," said Kerry.

Battersea Dogs Home was full of dogs. Mr Martin explained about Angus and a woman took them to the kennels*. "These dogs came in yesterday and today. I'll come with you," she said. They walked along the kennels. "People bring us about 700 dogs every Christmas," she explained. "Many were Christmas presents. Some people change their minds* about their new dogs after Christmas. So they leave them on a motorway or in a park. And then people find them and bring them here."
Kerry was shocked*. "That's really terrible!" she said. "How can they do that to a poor dog?" They walked past hundreds of dogs but they couldn't find Angus. At last, in the last kennel, they found him. Angus barked.
"I can see he's your dog," the woman said. "He's very lucky*. His owner loves him." She opened the kennel and Angus ran out.
"Yes," said Kerry. Then very, very quietly she said to Angus, "Sorry, old friend."

Christmas = *Weihnachten;* kitchen = *Küche;* Common = *Park, offene Landschaft im Stadtgebiet;* bark = *bellen;* threw = *warf;* tree = *Baum;* kennels = *Zwinger;* change their minds = *ändern ihre Meinung;* shocked = *schockiert;* He's very lucky = *Er hat großes Glück*

EASTENDERS

The car stopped. Mark Sampson looked at the old houses and empty factories. There weren't many cars on Bow Road that Sunday morning. But Mark didn't want to be in the East End*. His mother looked at him. "I'm sure you're going to like them all. Amanda is thirteen, too. And she's very pretty*." But Mark wanted to be back home in Clacton with his friends.

"We're almost there now," said Mark's father. "It only took an hour and a quarter from Clacton to here."

"Yes, here we are," said Mrs Sampson. She read the sign: Addington Road. Their new friends, Mr and Mrs Walters, lived at number 9 with their two children, Amanda and Lucy. Mr and Mrs Sampson met them in Spain in the summer. Mark wasn't with his parents in Spain – he spent his holiday at an adventure camp* in England.

Five minutes later they were sitting on the sofa in the living-room* of the Walters' small house. There were tea and biscuits on the table.

"What's this part of London called?" asked Mark. "Just the East End?"

"No, this is Bow," answered Amanda. "It's *in* the East End. The tube station is at the end of the road. I go to school by tube." She looked very important when she said it.

"By tube? I'm sure that's fun. I walk to school," said Mark.

Before lunch they all went for a walk. Outside in the street a black man was cleaning his car.

"You aren't cleaning that car again, are you, Vincent?" Mrs Walters smiled when she spoke.

"Well, somebody has got to have a clean car in this road, you know. Look at your old thing." Vincent smiled too.

"These are our friends from Clacton," said Mr Walters.

"Oh, yes. Nice to meet you," said Vincent.

They said goodbye and started to walk up the road.

"Are all the neighbours* nice?" asked Mrs Sampson.

"Well, I like most of them. Good morning, Mrs Mir. Is your shop open?" Mr Walters asked an old Indian* woman. She was wearing a very long dress. It was red and blue, green and brown and yellow.

"Yes, we're open. What would you like?" Mr Walters went in and bought some milk. Mrs Walters talked about the Mir family.

"Mr and Mrs Mir came here from India* 25 years ago. They couldn't speak very good English then. But their children have always lived here. Some things in the shop are more expensive, but it's open till 9 every evening. All the other shops are closed then."

"Have you got any British neighbours?" asked Mark.

Amanda looked at him. "Don't be silly," she said. "They are British."

"Amanda is right," said Mrs Walters. "Lots of our neighbours – or their families – came here from different* countries many years ago. But they're British."

After lunch the afternoon went quickly. Soon the Sampsons had to go home. Amanda suddenly asked Mark, "Are you going to visit us again soon?"

"I hope so," said Mark. The words* came quickly.

On the journey back home, Mark's mother smiled at him. "So you want to come here again soon, do you?" she asked. "You said you weren't interested in the East End."

"Well," said Mark, "the East End isn't very nice, but the people are interesting."

"Yes," said Mrs Sampson, "especially* the girls!"

East End = *älterer Wohn- und Industriebezirk im Osten Londons;* pretty [ˈprɪtɪ] = *hübsch;* camp = *Ferienlager;* living-room = *Wohnzimmer;* neighbour [ˈneɪbə] = *Nachbar(in);* Indian = *indisch;* India = *Indien;* different = *verschieden;* word = *Wort;* especially = *insbesondere*

FULHAM GIRL

Six-thirty.
"Oh, no!" thought Anna Looms. "It's still dark and the others are still asleep, but I've got to get up. It isn't fair."
Burnfoot Avenue was very quiet that morning. It was always quiet when Anna got up, but she could hear the cars in Fulham Road and Fulham Palace Road. She put on her clothes and went downstairs*.
She was quiet in the kitchen. Her mother hadn't got to get up till half past seven. She didn't start work in the launderette* till nine. So Anna had her breakfast alone. She loved her coffee and cornflakes. Coffee and cornflakes was a good start to her day.
She looked at the time. It was seven o'clock. Time to go. Outside it was raining again. The weather was terrible that winter and Anna hated it. She found her raincoat* and opened the door. She started her paper round* every morning at seven o'clock. She jumped on to her bike and said, "Hurry up, hurry up, Anna! You're late." Soon she was at Mr Patel's newspaper shop.

The paper round was fun. There were only four roads. Fulham was getting up. At one house a woman opened the door and fetched her milk.
"Hallo, Anna. It's ducks'* weather today," she said with a smile and Anna forgot the rain.
There were lights in some houses and others were dark. In Fulham Palace Road a few people were waiting for buses.
When Anna finished she went back home. Her mother was already downstairs. She was drinking a cup of tea. She never ate breakfast. Grandad was still in bed. He never got up till ten. Or even eleven. Then he drank tea and smoked and watched TV. He loved the horse races on TV. In the afternoons he watched the races and waited for his evening meal.
It wasn't raining now, but everything was wet. The cars were noisy on the wet roads. Anna's bike made a noise on them, too, when she was riding it to school. It only took ten minutes.

She went to a big comprehensive school. The boys and girls had a black and white and grey uniform*.

"What a uniform for a grey day like this!" thought Anna.

That day she had English and French and Geography and Maths and P. E. and History and Home Economics. All in one day!

"Too many lessons," she thought. But she liked most of them. Except for French. She didn't like the French teacher. English was OK and Geography was her favourite. After Maths she had lunch at school. In P. E. they played football and volleyball, and Anna liked both sports. In History she learned about King John, and Home Economics was all about breakfast. That was just right for Anna. She loved her breakfast. After school she didn't go home. She stayed at school for the photo club. She had an old camera. It was her father's. But he didn't live with the family now. The club met every Friday in the Science room. There was a dark room*, too, and the children learned a lot. They took lots of photos and Anna put the best photos on her wall at home.

After school in the summer Anna played outside with her friends. But it was winter now and dark at five. So she couldn't play street hockey or ride her skateboard in the quiet road. She had her evening meal and did all her homework. It wasn't too hard today. When it was hard she always thought: "We get too much homework. But the teachers don't think so." Then she watched TV and talked to grandad and helped her mother in the kitchen. And later, in bed, she listened to her radio. The weather forecast promised* a fine day tomorrow.

"That's good," thought Anna. "But it's still going to be dark at six-thirty."

downstairs = *unten, nach unten;* launderette [lɔːn'dret] = *Waschsalon;* raincoat = *Regenmantel;* do a paper round = *Zeitungen austragen;* duck = Ente; dark room = *Dunkelkammer;* promise = *versprechen*

HYDE PARK AND THE COLD COKE

Carol and Linda lived in Dover. In the summer holidays they went on a day trip to London. Their first stop was Buckingham Palace. There were lots of French, German, Italian and British coaches and hundreds of tourists. Carol and Linda listened to the German tourists. They could understand a few things. Linda took a photo of the palace and then the two girls walked to Hyde Park. There were hundreds of people there, too, but the park was enormous. They saw joggers, people with dogs and people on horses. Carol and Linda went out in a boat on the Serpentine, the big lake in Hyde Park. After the boat trip they sat on the grass and ate their sandwiches.
"I'd like a coke. A cold coke," said Linda.

Carol went to a restaurant and bought two cokes. They took the cokes to the lake. Near them there were two Jamaican* families. They all had long black hair and clothes of many colours. They were listening to music on an enormous cassette-recorder. The music was noisy but nice. Carol didn't want to sit near them, but Linda said, "Let's sit here. Then we can listen to their music."

The sun was warm and the lake was full of boats. Carol took a photo of Linda, and Linda took a photo of Carol. Then the girls opened their cokes. Carol played with the ring-pull*. Then she suddenly jumped up. There was blood on her hand.
"My finger! Ouch*, I've cut* my finger on the ring-pull!" There was a lot of blood. Linda was worried.

"What can we do?" she thought. Then one of the Jamaican men came to them.
"What's the matter*?" he asked.
"My friend has had an accident," said Linda. "She has cut her finger."
The man looked at Carol's finger.

"Oh, dear," he said. "That isn't very nice. I'll get my bag." He came back quickly and opened his bag. "I'll look after this cut for you," he said and then he looked at Linda. "Don't worry," he said. "I'm a nurse*. My name is Max."
"I'm Linda ," said Linda. "And this is my friend Carol."
"Now, Carol," said Max. "I'm going to put a plaster on your finger. Where do you come from? London?"
"No, Dover," said Carol.
"Well," said Max. "This plaster is OK for today. But you've got to see your

doctor in Dover tomorrow. OK?"
"Yes, OK, Mr – er ...," said Carol.
"Call me Max," said the Jamaican man. "Hey, come and sit with us and listen to the music. Then you can forget about your finger."

The two girls went and sat with the Jamaicans. They talked to them and listened to the music. They were really friendly people. Carol and Linda spent the afternoon with them. They took photos of everybody. At last, the girls had to go. They got up and said goodbye to their new friends.
"Bye, bye," said Max. "And don't forget! Go to your doctor tomorrow!"
"OK, Max. Bye, everybody!" Carol and Linda walked back to Victoria Station and waited for the train to Dover.
"Those Jamaicans were really nice," said Carol. "And I didn't want to sit near them. How silly of me!"

Jamaican = *Jamaikaner(in), jamaikanisch;* ring-pull = *Dosenverschluß;* Ouch! [aʊtʃ] = *Aua!;* cut = *schneiden;* What's the matter? = *Was ist los?;* nurse = *Krankenpfleger, Krankenschwester*

INDIAN FOOD – THE JEWEL OF KASHMIR

Jochen Keller was on a school trip to London. He was staying with Tony Clees and his family.
"I'm hungry," said Tony one evening after they came home from the cinema.
"Have you ever tried Indian food, Jochen?" asked Mrs Clees.
"No, never," said Jochen.
"OK," said Mr Clees. "Let's have an Indian takeaway."
"What's a 'takeaway'?" asked Jochen.
"You buy a bag of food in a restaurant. Then you take it away and eat it at home," said Mr Clees.
"Indian food," said Jochen, "does that mean curry*?"
"Yes, with lots of spices*. We'll get some," said Mr Clees, "and you can try it. Indian food is very popular in this country. And it isn't expensive."
Mr Clees gave Tony some money and the two boys left the house.

The Indian restaurant was called "The Jewel of Kashmir". They went in and an Indian waiter* came to them.
"Good evening. Yes, please?" he said.
"We'd like a takeaway, please," said Tony.
"Yes, I'll bring you a menu*," said the waiter.
The restaurant was one big room with about twenty tables. There were pictures of Kashmir on the red walls. Three Indian men and two Indian women worked there. The men had British clothes but the women had long Indian skirts and open shoes. The boys could hear Indian music.
The waiter brought* them a menu. Jochen looked at it.
"I don't know any of these dishes*," he said. "Do you?"
"I know some of them," answered Tony. "Look, this dish is an egg curry and this is a meat curry. What would you like?" he asked.
"Don't get me a meal, Tony. Can I try some of your food? Is that OK?" asked Jochen.
"OK," said Tony and ordered* three Indian meals. "Oh, and can we have four popadoms, please?" he said.
"What are they? What do you call them – popa..?" asked Jochen.
"Popadoms," said the waiter. "They're like big crisps. They're nice."
"How long is the food going to take?" asked Jochen.

"About fifteen to twenty minutes," said the waiter.

After a quarter of an hour the waiter arrived with the food in two bags.
Tony paid* and the boys left the restaurant. Five minutes later, they were back home. They put the bags on the table and took out the food.
"There are only three curries here. Didn't you want a meal, Jochen?" asked Mr Clees.
"I'm going to try some of Tony's curry," said Jochen. Tony gave him some food and Jochen tried it.
"Well? Do you like it?" asked Mrs Clees.
"Mmm, it's fine," said Jochen and ate some more. Two minutes later, he jumped up from the table.
"What's the matter?" asked Tony.
"Water*! Can I have some water, please?" said Jochen.
"No, not water, Jochen. Eat some yoghurt. That's better than water," said Mr Clees and gave Jochen some yoghurt.
"Don't worry. We all started like that," said Tony.
"You've got to practise with Indian takeaways," laughed Mrs Clees.

curry = *Curry, Currygericht;* spice = *Gewürz;* waiter = *Kellner;* menu = *Speisekarte;* brought = *brachte;* dish = *Gericht;* order = *bestellen;* paid = *bezahlte;* water = *Wasser*

LONDON FOR FREE

"Well, what now?" asked Neil when they came out of the London Transport Museum. He had no more money. Now he just had his day ticket for the Underground and the buses. So he could get back home to Brixton all right. Clare still had £3.50 and Jonjo £1.
"£4.50 isn't too bad," said Clare. She tried to smile but it wasn't a very good smile. £4.50 wasn't very much really. Their tall friend, Jonjo, said nothing. He was thinking. The other two looked at him. Perhaps he had an idea.
"We want to stay in town till the evening, OK?" said Jonjo. "Well, £4.50 is enough for some food and a drink. And there are a lot of free things to do in London."
"Like what then?" asked Clare.
Jonjo explained: "Right, listen ..."

They looked at the bus map. They got it free from the Covent Garden Underground station.
"Well, where's this museum?" asked Neil.
Jonjo answered: "It's in the City, I think. Yes, there it is."
"And it's really free?" Neil didn't think so but Jonjo was sure.
Clare didn't want to go to another museum. One was enough for her on one day. She wasn't interested in the history of London. She wanted to listen to some music. Neil liked music, too. He was a reggae fan.
"Well, we're already in the right place for some music," said Jonjo.
Half an hour later the three friends from Brixton were in a big crowd* at Covent Garden. Four street singers were singing "Bye, bye, love", an old hit. The crowd loved them.
At the end of the song the street singers collected money from the crowd. It was their last song for the day. Jonjo went and talked to one of them.
"I'm sorry," he said, "but we haven't got very much money. We can't give you anything."
"That's OK. We know what that's like. For people without much money the show is free. OK?"
Jonjo said thank you and returned to his friends. "They're really nice."

Neil thought they were terrific, not just nice. He said it four or five times. "Terrific!"

"But I thought you only liked reggae, Neil," said Clare. Then she spoke to Jonjo. "That was a really good idea, Jonjo. Thanks. Now we can go to that museum."

It was five stops on the tube to the Barbican. They had to go there via* King's Cross. In the Museum of London the three friends walked through* the history of the city from 250,000 years ago to today. There were shops and buildings and rooms and lots of other things from many different times. They could go into them, look at them, touch them, use them. It was like a journey into the past*. In a dark room they listened to the story* of the Great Fire* of London in 1666 and the old city burnt* in front of* their eyes*.

When they came out again, at half past three, Clare said,"That was the best museum I've ever been to. And it's free. That's just great. Why aren't all museums free?" She wanted to come back next weekend. Two hours was not enough time.

Jonjo was hungry. So they found the nearest hamburger restaurant and spent their £4.50.

It was four o'clock when they came out of the restaurant. They took the tube to Kensington High Street , walked along the High Street for half an hour and looked at the shop windows. They couldn't buy anything in the expensive shops, but just looking was fun, too. Then Clare saw the time. It was almost half past five. She had to be home at half past six, so it was time to go.

"I didn't know it before, but you can have a really good time in London without much money," she said. "– When you're with your friends." Neil and Jonjo smiled at her. She took their hands and they started their journey back to Brixton.

crowd = *Menschenmenge;* via = *über;* through = *durch;* past = *Vergangenheit;* story = *Geschichte;* fire = *Brand, Feuer;* burnt = *brannte;* in front of = *vor;* eyes = *Augen*

THE MUSICAL NEIGHBOUR

"There it is," said Alan. He pointed to the big cinema. "See. We aren't late."
The film started at 3.35 but the three friends arrived at Leicester Square* half an hour before that.
"We've got time for a coffee," said Linda.
"Terrific idea!" Jason smiled. But Alan had another idea.
"Let's buy the tickets first. We can have a drink after that. Come on." So they all walked towards the cinema.
"Oh, no!" Alan said. "Look at that!" At the cinema a sign said:
"Queue* here for 'Superman'." And the queue was already 50 metres long. They went to the end of it.
"Well, we can forget about that coffee then," said Jason. "Look at the queue! I don't think we're going to get a ticket."
Near the end of the queue a man in white was selling hot dogs* and hamburgers. He looked at Jason and laughed. "Don't worry. The cinema is big enough for you, too."
"Wait a minute, have you got drinks?" Linda asked him.
"Yes, of course," he answered.
"We'll have ..." But Jason couldn't finish. A big drum* went, "Boom, boom, boom." A tall man with a rubber mask* came along the road. He had an old black hat*, a green T-shirt, long red trousers and big blue shoes. He had a big drum and a lot of other instruments.

For the next ten minutes Jason, Alan and Linda forgot about their drinks. They forgot about the film and forgot about the queue. The man with the clown's* mask played his instruments and sang. He made jokes and talked to the people in the queue. They all laughed.
"Isn't he good!" said Alan. Then the funny man walked along the queue again with his old black hat in his hand. Lots of people put money into the hat and the man said, "Thank you very much. Thank you."
The three friends each gave him 10p when he got to the end of the queue. "Terrific. Just terrific," said Alan.
"Thanks." The man in the mask took off his instruments.

"One hamburger with lots of ketchup – right?" asked the hot dog man.
"That's right," answered the clown. Then he took off his rubber mask and smiled.
"Hallo, Linda. What are you doing in the centre of London?"
It was Barry Wilton, her brother's friend. He lived in the same street.
Linda couldn't believe* it. "Paul was talking about you last week," she said. "He said, 'My friend Barry is never going to get a good job. He's just a clown.' – He doesn't know how right he is."
"Well, I didn't want to work in an office when I left school," said Barry. "Not like Paul. This is much more fun."
"Have you done it for long?" Jason wanted to know.
"About six months now."
"Do you make much money?" Alan asked.

Barry finished his hamburger and thought for a few seconds. Then he looked in his hat and smiled. "Well, it's OK. It isn't going to make me rich*, but it's enough. And I've only just started work today. Most people had to start six hours ago. Look."

On Barry's big blue watch it was 3.30.

"I don't want to go to work when it's cold in the morning or raining. And I haven't got to. I can just stay in bed. But it's nice today. That's why I'm here. I've got work to do now." Then he put the drum on again. He looked at Linda one more time with his mask in his hands.

"Why have you got that mask?" she asked him.

"Well, it makes me different from other street singers. And people like you don't know me when I'm playing. This job isn't easy when people know you. Bye."

The drum started again. "Boom, boom, boom." Barry went and the queue suddenly started to move.

"Well, what about that*! Your brother isn't going to believe it," Alan said to Linda.

She laughed and answered, "Yes. Barry really is a clown – a very good clown, too."

square = *Platz;* queue [kjuː] = *sich anstellen, Schlange stehen; Schlange;* hot dog = *Würstchen mit Brötchen;* drum = *Trommel;* rubber mask = *Gummimaske;* hat = *Hut;* believe = *glauben;* rich = *reich;* What about that! = *Das ist ein Ding!*

OXFORD STREET PRICES

"Only two more presents and then we've got something for everybody," said Susan. The two sisters walked along Oxford Street. Jane had four Christmas presents in her bag. They needed two more things, one for their mother and one for their grandmother. The shops in Oxford Street were very full at this time of the year. There were only five shopping days till Christmas.

The two girls stopped at Selfridges, one of the big department stores in Oxford Street.
"Let's go in here," said Jane. "They've got lots of nice things."
After ten minutes, Susan saw something. It was a cup with a picture of Prince Charles and Princess Diana.
"Look, this is just right for mum's breakfast tea," said Susan. "She likes Charles and Di."

"Now we've got something for everybody except grandma," said Jane.
The girls left Selfridges and walked on. They passed* a small shop. It was full of people. The owner was standing at a big table. He was telling jokes and people were laughing.
"Let's look in here," said Jane. "Perhaps we can find the last present."

The girls pushed* into the shop and listened to the owner. He had a model of the Tower of London in his hand.
"And here we have a model of the Tower," he said. "It has a radio and a light in it. Just right for a Christmas present."
"Hey, that's great!" Jane said to Susan. "That's just right for grandma. Then she can listen to the radio in bed."
"Come along*, everybody," said the owner of the shop. "I'm not asking for twelve pounds. I'm not asking for ten pounds. I'm not even asking for eight pounds. You can have this model of the Tower with a radio and a light for only six pounds fifty pence. Hurry up, now, I can't wait all day. Yes, here you are*. Six pounds fifty. I've only got five of them. Who's next?"
"Let's buy one," said Susan to Jane. "It's really cheap."

"Don't pay Oxford Street prices," said a man near Susan. "That thing isn't worth six pounds fifty. Go to Tottenham Court Road. You can buy your presents there for half the price."

Susan and Jane weren't sure. They waited and thought about it. But then the shop owner sold the last Tower.
"Well, that's that*," said Susan. "I wanted to buy a Tower, and now he has sold them all."
"Let's go to Tottenham Court Road," said Jane. "Perhaps we can find something there." After twenty minutes they arrived at Tottenham Court Road. The shops there were all TV and hi-fi shops.
"No," said Susan, "we'll never find a present here. Let's get the bus home and try again tomorrow."

They waited at a bus-stop. It started to rain. At last the bus arrived. The girls got on the bus. When the bus stopped at the next bus-stop Jane looked in a shop window.
"Come on, Susan! Get off the bus! Quickly!" she said.
"Why?" asked Susan.
"Look, there in that shop window!" said Jane. Susan looked. There, at the back* of the window, was the same model of the Tower of London. A card said, "Souvenir* of London with radio and light. Only £3.50."

pass = *vorbeigehen an;* push = *sich drängen, schieben;* Come along = *Treten Sie näher;* Here you are = *Bitte schön;* That's that = *Das war's;* at the back = *hinten;* souvenir = *Andenken*

A Quick River Swim

"Tim! Come here, please," said Mrs Bates. Tim came out of the telephone box and went back to the other pupils from Queenswood School.
"Now, we're going to get on our boat in two minutes. We're all going on a trip to the Thames Barrier*. After that we're going to visit the famous Cutty Sark."
"Please, Mrs Bates. What's the Cutty Sark?" asked one girl.
"It's an old ship. We'll find out more later," said the teacher.
"I've already seen the Thames Barrier," said Tim to his friend Derek. "It's boring."
"When did you go?" asked Derek.
"Last month. On my birthday," said Tim. "Please, Miss! Can't we go swimming? I've already seen all that."
"Don't be silly, Tim! We haven't got our swimming things. Now, we can spend an hour at the Thames Barrier and an hour at the Cutty Sark," said Mrs Bates. "Here's our boat now." The boat arrived at Westminster Pier*. Thirty noisy pupils climbed on to the boat. It left the pier and the guide* on the boat spoke to them.
"Good afternoon, girls and boys from Queenswood School," he said. "Your trip to the Thames Barrier takes an hour and a half. The journey from there to the Cutty Sark takes another twenty-five minutes."

After ninety minutes, they all arrived at the Thames Barrier.
"Who can tell me why this Barrier is here?" asked Mrs Bates.
"It protects* London from sea floods*," said one of the girls.
"Very good," said the teacher. "Now we're going to go into the Visitor Centre and see a film about the building* work. We're going to do a class project on the Thames Barrier. And I want the best class project in Queenswood School from this class."
"Boring," said Tim. "I've seen it all."
In the Centre the class saw a film about the Barrier. Everybody thought it was really interesting – except Tim.

After an hour, they got back on the boat. The guide told the class about the famous ship, the Cutty Sark.
"This ship brought tea from China and India to London a hundred years ago."

Soon, the boat stopped at Greenwich Pier near the Cutty Sark. The pupils liked the old ship. It was black and white and very tidy. Tim climbed a rope* and the

attendant* was angry with him. Mrs Bates sent him off the ship and he had to wait outside.

When the class left the ship, Tim wasn't there.
"Oh, no, where's that boy?" said Mrs Bates.
"Mrs Bates! Come quickly!" called Derek. "Tim is in the Thames!" Mrs Bates and the pupils ran to the river. Three people were pulling Tim out of the water.
"Tim!" said Mrs Bates. "What happened*?"
Tim was very frightened. He was crying* and his pullover, his jeans and his hair were all wet and full of mud.
"I tried to walk along the wall," he said. "And then I just fell."
An attendant took Tim into her office and brought him a cup of tea. "Can his parents come and get him?" the attendant asked. "And bring some dry things? His clothes are still wet."
"Well," said Derek. "Tim wanted to go swimming today. Now he has done it."

Thames Barrier = *Sturmflutsperre an der Themse;* pier = *Anlegestelle;* guide = *Führer(in);* protect = *schützen, abschirmen;* sea flood = *Überschwemmung durch Sturmflut;* build = *bauen;* rope = *Seil, Tau;* attendant = *Aufseher(in);* happen = *passieren, geschehen;* cry = *weinen*

THE TOWER – BY UNDERGROUND OR VIA BANK?

They saw the big red bus when they got to the end of Portobello Road. They tried to run, but it was difficult.

"I've never seen so many people. But it's terrific, isn't it?"

Belinda laughed. Yes, London was great and the market* in Portobello Road was even better. And Saturday was always her favourite day.

"Come on. Hurry up," said her friend Clive. "It's a number 15. We can get it."

"Yes, but is it the right bus? It says East Ham on it," asked Belinda.

"Of course it is. It's a number 15. I'm from London, you know. I know the buses for the Tower." But Belinda wasn't sure. She really wanted to go by tube. She loved the Underground. There wasn't one in Swansea, where she lived.

They got to the bus just in time. Belinda only had one more day in London and she wanted to see the Tower. On Sunday evening she had to get the train back to Swansea. Her friend, Clive, was from Tottenham.

"I know London well," he said to her when she arrived. "I've always lived here." Belinda wanted to see all the sights, so she was happy about that.

They sat upstairs* in the number 15. After a few minutes Belinda pointed. They could see Paddington Station, where she arrived. She looked at her friend with her big blue eyes. "That's where I'm leaving from tomorrow."

"Oh, no," he thought. "She's going to cry." He smiled at her. He was sorry that she had to leave tomorrow. They both looked out of the window and said nothing.

"Fares*, please." The conductor* came upstairs. He looked at their Travelcards* and they looked out of the window again.

There was busy Oxford Street, full of shops and people. The bus stopped and a woman with a small child came upstairs. Before they found a seat the bus suddenly started again The child fell and the woman dropped her shopping bag. Lots of things fell out. The child was crying and Clive and Belinda helped them.

"These buses! They're terrible sometimes," said the woman to Clive and Belinda. "Thank you so much."

Belinda looked at the hundreds of Saturday morning tourists at Piccadilly Circus and Trafalgar Square. Then the bus went on into the City.

"There's the Bank of England," said Clive suddenly. Belinda thought about all the money there. The conductor was upstairs again. He wanted money, too – from the new passengers*. "Fares, please. Any more fares please. Thank you." He stopped next to them.

"Whereyougoin?" he asked. Belinda often didn't understand these Londoners. It was easy for Clive.

"To the Tower," he answered. "We're almost there, aren't we?"

The conductor just laughed. "The Tower? Wrong bus, friend."

"But the number 15 goes to the Tower, doesn't it?" Clive asked.

"Some number 15s go to the Tower. Yes. But not this bus."

"Well, why not?" Clive didn't understand.

"Didn't you see the sign?" asked the conductor. "East Ham – via Bank?"

"Yes," said Clive. "What about it*?" "Well, buses via Bank don't go to the Tower. It isn't the same way. You want a bus for East Ham - via Tower." Belinda looked at Clive. He was very red. "Didn't you know that? You're a Londoner," she asked him. He didn't answer but looked at the bus conductor for help. The conductor smiled and said, "OK. I can tell you the way to the Tower."

They got off the bus at the next stop. That was Aldgate. They went into the Underground station and took the tube to Tower Hill. The two friends spent the afternoon at the Tower of London. Belinda loved it. When they left, Belinda bought some postcards for her family and friends in Swansea. Now it was time to go home. Outside the Tower Clive said, "I know the way home. We get a bus to ..." But Belinda stopped him. She took his hand and said, "No more buses. We're going by tube." And the girl from Swansea took the London boy home to Tottenham.

market = *Markt;* upstairs = *oben, nach oben;* fare = *Fahrgeld;* conductor = *Schaffner(in);* Travelcard = *Tageskarte, Wochenkarte;* passenger = *Fahrgast;* What about it? = *Was ist damit?*

WITH XY TO THE ZOO

Julie tried one last time.
"Let's go to the London Dungeon* on our trip, Valerie. Please."
"Julie, all the group* wants to go to Kew Gardens," said Valerie, the youth club leader, "and then to London Zoo. So we aren't going to the London Dungeon. OK?"
"But I don't like plants and I don't like animals." Julie was still trying.
"But lots of other people like them, Julie. We're all going to have a lot of fun, I'm sure. You, too."

One week later Valerie was walking next to Julie when they left Kew Gardens.
"Well, Julie, do you still not like plants?" she asked.
The girl thought for a minute. "I liked one plant," she answered. "The Venus Fly Trap*. Because it catches* things and eats them." Julie laughed. "Can you buy them in the shops?"
Valerie had to laugh, too. Sometimes Julie was very funny.
The group from the XY Youth Club travelled on the Underground from Kew to Paddington. From there it was a five minute walk to Little Venice, where they got on the boat.
Julie read about the boat trip.
"Our trip takes us along the Regent's Canal*. We start in Little Venice, near Paddington. On the way we see Regent's Park and go through London Zoo. After that we arrive at Camden Lock*. The trip takes about one and a half hours. – What? One and a half hours! Oh, no!"
"What's wrong now, Julie?" asked Valerie.
"One and a half hours on this, this ..."
"You can see the sights better from a boat, Julie."
But Julie didn't want to know. She thought for a minute. Then she asked her next question. "Are we going to stop at the zoo?"
"No, we aren't," said Valerie, "this boat doesn't stop till Camden Lock. Then it's a fifteen minute walk back to the zoo."
"You mean we go right through the zoo but don't stop? Then we've got to walk there? That's silly!" said the girl.

"We all want to see Camden Lock, Julie. It's very interesting." Valerie went to talk to the others.
"Well, I'm not walking to the zoo," thought Julie. Then she got up and went to the back of the boat.

Valerie counted* the group when they got off the boat. Fifteen. She counted them again. There were still only fifteen. But sixteen started the trip in Little Venice.
"What's wrong?" asked one of the girls.

"I'm not sure. Wait a minute," she said to her group. "There are only fifteen of us. Who ...?"
She didn't finish her question. One of the boys said, "It's Julie. She isn't here. She jumped on to the path* when we went past that boat near the zoo."

Julie stood* on the path. She could hear animals but she couldn't see them. She didn't understand it. A man was walking along the path. Perhaps he could help her. "This is the zoo, isn't it?" she asked.
"Well, that's the zoo," he said and pointed at the wall next to the path, "and that's the zoo." This time he pointed to the other side* of the canal. "But you can't get in here."
Julie didn't understand. She asked another question.
"You mean I'm not in the zoo?" She didn't like this very much.
"No. It's a long walk to where you go in." The old man pointed again. "That way, I think. Along the canal."
Julie thought, "Oh, no! Why am I always so silly?" and began to walk along the path. After some time she came to a bridge. When she was on the bridge she saw the others. Valerie just smiled at her and asked her, "Have you had a nice long walk, too, Julie?"
At first Julie didn't answer but then she started to smile, too.
"We can go to the London Dungeon next time," said Valerie. "But now let's go into the zoo – together."

dungeon ['dʌndʒn] = *Kerker;* group = *Gruppe;* Venus Fly Trap = *Venusfliegenfalle;* catch = *fangen;* canal [kə'næl] = *Kanal;* lock = *Schleuse;* count = *zählen;* path = *Weg;* stood = *stand;* side = *Seite*

After the stories ...

Airport to New Cross

A Find the words. The letters in boxes give you another word from the text.

1 There was a poster on the – – ❑ – – – – –.
(pl**A**tform - A)
2 Heathrow is fifteen – ❑ – – – west of London.
3 The Pattersons went into the – – ❑ – – – – – building.
4 Mr Patterson needed a – – – – ❑ – – – –.
5 – ❑ – – – – is the biggest city in England.
6 The tube is an underground ❑ – – – – – –.
7 The Pattersons bought four ❑ – – – – – –.

B 1 Where did the Pattersons fly from?
2 When did they arrive at London Heathrow?
3 Where's New Cross?
4 Who was waiting at New Cross station?
5 How long did the tube journey take?

C How many words can you make from H E A T H R O W A I R P O R T ?
Try to write 15 words in five minutes.
Examples: that, throw.

D Chain Game.
You're going to New York and you've got to put things in your bags.
The first pupil says, "I'm putting jeans in my bag."
The second pupil says, "I'm putting jeans and a T-shirt in my bag."
The third pupil says, "I'm putting jeans, a T-shirt and ..."

E London is 40 miles (60 km) from east to west.
Make a list of places 40 miles from your home.
How long does it take to get there by bike/car/bus/train?

Battersea Christmas Dogs

A That's wrong. But what's right?

1 The Martins always have lunch at 2 o'clock on Christmas Day.
The Martins always have lunch at ...
2 Angus is a black Scottish terrier.
3 Kerry threw a ball and it flew over the lake.
4 Kerry wanted to watch a film in the evening.
5 People bring about 100 dogs to the Dogs Home at Christmas.
6 Angus wasn't at the Dogs Home.

B Who said this?

1 "I'll take Angus for a walk."
2 "I can see he's your dog."
3 "Don't be late home."
4 "I'm going to Battersea Dogs Home."
5 "Come here, boy."

C What happened at these times?
1 Christmas Day, 10 o'clock
2 Christmas Day, 1 o'clock
3 Christmas Day after dinner
4 the next morning

D Can you say why ...
1 Kerry took Angus for a walk?
2 Angus liked Tooting Bec Common?
3 Kerry was worried in the evening?
4 Kerry was shocked at the Dogs Home?

E How many words can you make from C H R I S T M A S P R E S E N T ?
Try to find 20 words in five minutes.
Examples: this, car.

F Talk about presents with a partner. What would you like for Christmas/for your birthday?

G What's Christmas like in your family?

Eastenders

A Who said this?
1 "I go to school by tube."
2 "I'm sure that's fun."
3 "Nice to meet you."
4 "Is your shop open?"
5 "Don't be silly."
6 "We're almost there now."
7 "Here we are."
8 "They're British."

B Find 9 words from the text.

E	**L**	**U**	**N**	**C**	**H**	A	Y	C	L	E	A	N	F	D	I
F	F	E	R	E	N	T	F	F	P	R	E	T	T	Y	M
I	L	K	F	H	O	L	I	D	A	Y	D	A	F	C	A
R	A	P	A	R	K	A	N	E	I	G	H	B	O	U	R

C 1 Why are the Sampsons going to London?
2 Where did they meet the Walters?
3 How do Mark and Amanda get to school?
4 Why is Vincent cleaning his car?
5 How long is Mrs Mir's shop open?

D Complete the sentences.
1 Mark Sampson didn't want to be in the ...
2 His mother said, "I'm sure ..."
3 The Walters ...
4 Before lunch they all ...
5 Mrs Mir's shop is open till ...
6 On their way home Mark said, "The people are ..."

E Who ...
1 came from India 25 years ago?
2 went to Spain?
3 walks to school?
4 often cleans his car?
5 enjoyed the visit to the East End?

F 1 How do you go to school?
2 What are your neighbours like?
3 Would you like to go on holiday without your parents? Why/Why not?

Fulham Girl

A That's wrong. But what's right?
1 Anna has breakfast with her mother.
2 Anna has tea for breakfast.
3 Her paper round starts at 6.30.
4 Lots of people were waiting for their buses.
5 Anna likes all her lessons.
6 Home Economics was about cornflakes.
7 After the photo club Anna played with her friends outside.

B What time was it when ...
1 Anna got up?
2 Anna started her paper round?
3 Anna's mother started work?
4 Anna's grandfather got up?
5 Anna had lunch at school?

C Find the words. The letters in boxes tell us something that Anna does.
1 The weather report ❑ – – – – – – – a fine day tomorrow.
2 Anna had coffee and – – – – – – ❑ – – – for breakfast.
3 Anna stayed at the school for the ❑ – – – – club.
4 She had an old – – – ❑ – –.
5 In the evening she did her – – – – – – ❑ –.
6 At school she had to wear a – – – – – ❑ –.
7 She put on her clothes and went – ❑ – – – – – – – –.
8 Geography was her – – – – ❑ – – – – subject.
9 Her mother worked at a – – – ❑ – – – – – – –
10 "It's ❑ – – – – weather today".

D Make a poster in English for a school club.
or
Anna has got to wear a uniform at school. Draw a uniform for your school (for boys or for girls).

Hyde Park and the Cold Coke

A Word snake. The last letter of one word is the first letter of the next word.
(SummeR, RaiN, NicE, E...)
1 Carol and Linda travelled to ...
2 Max is a ...
3 The park is ...

4 The girls went there in the ... holidays.
5 Carol bought two cokes at a ...
6 The girls went home by ...

B 1 Who lives in Dover?
2 Who was at Buckingham Palace?
3 Who bought cokes?
4 Who was listening to music?
5 Who played with a ring-pull?
6 Who put a plaster on Carol's finger?

C Tell the story.
Carol and Linda ...
One day they ...
At Buckingham Palace they ...
Later the two girls ...
Carol ...
Max ...
The Jamaicans ...
At the end of the afternoon Carol and Linda ...

D Think of a German word for:
Palace – enormous – grass – blood – jogger – day trip – plaster – doctor

E Make a poster for a park.

Welcome to ... **Open from ... till ...** **You can ...** **Please don't ...**

You can draw pictures on your poster, too.

Indian Food – The Jewel of Kashmir

A That's wrong. But what's right?
1 Jochen Keller stayed with an Indian family.
2 Mr Clees asked, "Have you ever tried Indian food?"
3 Indian food is very expensive.
4 The waiters at the restaurant had long Indian skirts.
5 Tony knew all the Indian dishes.
6 Jochen wanted a big meal.
7 Tony ordered four meals.
8 Mr Clees gave Jochen some water.

B Make a list of all the words in the text for things to eat or drink.

C Find 9 words from the text:

O	D	I	S	H	Y	O	F	O	O	D	R	Y	M	E	A
L	R	Y	O	G	H	U	R	T	C	U	R	R	Y	T	A
K	E	A	W	A	Y	O	Y	A	M	E	N	U	R	E	S
T	A	U	R	A	N	T	A	U	W	A	I	T	E	R	Y

D Who said this?
1 "I don't know any of these dishes."
2 "They're like big crisps."
3 "Let's have an Indian takeaway."
4 "What's the matter?"
5 "Have you ever tried Indian food?"
6 "We all started like that."

E Make a menu in English for a German meal for guests from Britain.

London for Free

A 1 How much money did Neil have?
2 What was Jonjo's idea?
3 Why didn't Claire want to go to another museum?
4 What story did they hear at the Museum of London?
5 Where did they go at 3.30?
6 Where do the three friends live?

B Who said this?
1 "I thought you only liked reggae."
2 "Let's go back to Covent Garden."
3 "Why aren't all museums free?"
4 "Well, what now?"
5 "£4.50 isn't too bad."
6 "We can't give you anything."

C Find the names of:
- two museums
- four Underground stations.

D Find the words. The first letters of the words make two words from the text.
1 One Underground station is Covent ...
2 Neil is a ... fan.
3 The friends want to stay in London till the ...
4 They didn't buy ... in the shops.
5 The London Underground is called the ...
6 Neil and Jonjo are Clare's ...
7 Clare wasn't ... in the history of London.
8 In the dark ... the city burned in front of their eyes.
9 The shops in Kensington High Street were ...

E Make a plan for a visitor to your town.
What can he/she do?
Can you think of some free things, too?

The Musical Neighbour

A Find the words. One letter from each word gives you a word from the text.
Example: qesura (1) = (square - **S**)
qesura (1) - equue (2) - alpy (1) - koje (4) - berrub (6)
neyom (1) - hebrumrag (2) - knird (4).

B Word snake. The last letter of one word is the first letter of the next word.
1 The tall man was wearing a rubber ...
2 Do you like hamburgers with ...?
3 There were lots of ... waiting in front of the cinema.
4 The three friends went to the ... of the queue.
5 Barry had a big ...
6 He was playing ... and singing.
7 Barry is a very good ...

C What happened first? And then? Put the sentences in the right order.
1 There was a big queue of people.
2 At 3 o'clock the three friends arrived at Leicester Square.
3 He made music and talked to the people.
4 Then Linda found out that the tall man was her brother's friend.
5 They wanted to see the film "Superman".
6 Suddenly they saw a tall man with a rubber mask and musical instruments.

D Who said this?
1 "Barry really is a clown."
2 "Look at that."
3 "It isn't going to make me rich."
4 "Terrific idea."
5 "He's just a clown."
6 "We've got time for a coffee."

E Draw a picture of Barry. (Look at lines 18-21 in the text.)

Oxford Street Prices

A Put the sentences in the right order.
1 But the girls didn't buy it.
2 Susan and Jane were walking along Oxford Street.
3 Suddenly they saw something nice in a shop window.
4 The owner sold models of the Tower.
5 But they still needed two more presents.
6 They bought a nice cup there.
7 They got on a bus to go home.
8 Then they found a small shop full of people.
9 First they went to Selfridges.
10 They went to Tottenham Court Road.
How does the story end? What do you think?

B The "present" game.
The first pupil says: "I'm giving a record to grandma."
The second pupil says: "I'm giving a record and a cake to grandma."

C Find 10 words from the text:

R	A	D	I	O	W	R	P	R	I	C	E	J	O	K
E	P	O	W	N	O	W	N	E	R	P	R	E	S	E
N	T	P	U	S	H	G	R	A	N	D	M	A	W	I
N	D	O	W	P	E	N	C	E	A	M	O	D	E	L

D What Christmas presents can you buy for your family?
I can buy ... for ...

E The shop owner was very good at selling things. (Look at lines 18-29.) Now try to sell something funny to the class:
10 baby rabbits,
a cup with Princess Diana on it,
...

F Make an advert in English for something. You can use pictures in your advert, too.

A Quick River Swim

A Find 10 words from the text.

A	B	B	A	R	R	I	E	R	D	E	P	I	E	R	A	T	T
E	N	D	A	N	T	E	P	R	O	J	E	C	T	L	Y	I	V
I	S	I	T	F	I	L	M	A	R	O	P	E	V	I	S	I	L
L	Y	I	V	I	T	R	I	P	F	L	O	O	D	I	N	G	Y

B That's wrong. But what's right?
1 The teacher told the pupils what the Cutty Sark was.
2 Tim's birthday was three months ago.
3 There were 25 pupils in the class.
4 The trip to the Thames Barrier took 60 minutes.
5 Tim thought the film was interesting.
6 Tim wanted to swim in the Thames.

C 1 Why did Tim think the Thames Barrier was boring?
2 How long was the journey from the Thames Barrier to the Cutty Sark?
3 What does the Thames Barrier do?
4 What's the Cutty Sark?
5 How did Tim get wet?

D Word snake. The last letter of one word is the first letter of the next word.
1 There was a ... Centre at the Barrier.
2 Tim climbed a ...
3 Everybody laughed – ... Tim.
4 The class went on a ... to the Thames Barrier.
5 The boat arrived at Westminster ...

E Mrs Bates phoned Tim's parents. Act the dialogue with a partner.

The Tower – by Underground or via Bank?

A Find all the places in London in the text. How many did you find?

B That's wrong. What's right? (Look at a map of Britain.)
1 Swansea is near London.
2 It isn't near the sea.
3 It's in the north of England.

C Word snake. The last letter of one word is the first letter of the next word.
1 There was a ... in Portobello Road.
2 Belinda thought it was ...

3 The ... came upstairs.
4 When the conductor said, "Wrong bus", Clive was very ...
5 Running was ... in Portobello Road.
6 Clive and Belinda took the tube to ... Hill.

D Find the right order.
1 Belinda loved the Tower.
2 On their way home Belinda showed Clive the way.
3 They sat upstairs and showed the conductor their Travelcards.
4 On Saturday Belinda and Clive wanted to see the Tower.
5 Then they found out that they were on the wrong bus.
6 Belinda bought photos for her family.
7 They took a number 15 bus.
8 So they got off and took the tube to the Tower.

E The tube game
Look at the Underground map with a partner. Ask questions. Your partner has got 20 seconds for his/her answer.
You: "I want to travel from ... to ... Have I got to change trains?"
Your partner: "Yes, you've got to change at .../No, you haven't."

With XY to the Zoo

A Find the words. The letters in boxes give you a place name from the text.
1 The Venus Fly Trap ❑ – – – – – – things.
2 The group got on the – – ❑ – at Little Venice.
3 It was a five ❑ – – – – – walk from Paddington.
4 After the boat trip Valerie – – – – – – ❑ the group.
5 – – – – ❑ didn't want to walk to the zoo.
6 From the path Julie couldn't see the – ❑ – – – – –.
7 Julie had to walk along the – – – – ❑.
8 She saw the ❑ – – – – – from the bridge.
9 Valerie was the youth ❑ – – – leader.
10 Julie had a long – – – ❑, too.

B 1 Why didn't Julie want to go to Kew Gardens?
2 Why did Julie like the Venus Fly Trap?
3 How long was the trip to Camden Lock?
4 How many pupils got off the boat at Camden Lock?
5 Why wasn't Julie there?

C Find the words. The letters in boxes give you another place name.
1 DRAELE ❑ – – – – –
2 SAMUFO – – – ❑ – –
3 LACNA – – ❑ – –
4 GREBID – – – ❑ – –
5 NUGEDON – – – – – ❑ –
6 REGNADS – – – – – ❑ –
7 OZO ❑ – –
8 TUENSOIQ – – – – – – ❑ –
9 NUTOC – ❑ – – –

D You've got three days in London. Make a plan of what you'd like to do.

Quiz

A Do you remember?
1 Who can stay in bed on cold mornings?
2 What did Anna's grandad do during the day?
3 What's the Cutty Sark?
4 How many times did the Pattersons change trains?
5 Who put a plaster on Carol's finger and what was his job?
6 How did Julie get to London Zoo?
7 Who was Mrs Mir?
8 Where did Neil and his friends spend £4.50?
9 Why did Susan and Jane go to Oxford Street?
10 Who said that yoghurt was better than water?
11 Why did Belinda and Clive get off the number 15 bus?
12 Where did Kerry find Angus?

B Answer the questions. Then find the places on the map on page 39.
1 Where did Linda and Carol meet the Jamaicans?
2 Where did Neil, Clare and Jonjo listen to street singers?
3 Where did Linda, Alan and Jason stand in a queue?
4 Where did Susan and Jane do their Christmas shopping?
5 Where did Clive and Belinda spend their Saturday afternoon?
6 Where did Valerie take the youth club?

C Look at the maps on pages 38 and 39. Find the names:
1 3 stations
2 2 parks
3 a river, a lake and a canal
4 an airport
5 2 museums
6 3 famous buildings

D Answer the questions and find the places on the map on page 38.
1 Where's the Dogs' Home?
2 Where did the Walters live?
3 Where did Mrs Bates take her class?
4 Where did Clive and Belinda go after their visit to the Tower?
5 Where did Valerie's group want to go?

E Look at the Underground map.
1 Which station is near the Tower?
2 Which stations are in Heathrow Airport?
3 Which lines is Covent Garden on?
4 How many lines go to Oxford Circus?
5 You're at Victoria Station and you want to go to Marble Arch. How can you get there?
6 You're at Hyde Park Corner. You want to go to the Museum of London. How can you get there? (*London for Free* gives you some important information).

List of Names

Aldgate ['ɔ:ldgeɪt]
Amanda [ə'mændə]
Barbican ['bɑ:bɪkn]
Battersea ['bætəsi:]
Belinda [bɪ'lɪndə]
Bow [bəʊ]
Camden Lock ['kæmdn 'lɒk]
Cindy ['sɪndɪ]
Covent Garden ['kɒvnt 'gɑ:dn]
Cutty Sark ['kʌtɪ 'sɑ:k]
Diana [daɪ'ænə]
East Ham ['i:st 'hæm]
Fulham ['fʊləm]
Greenwich ['grenɪtʃ]
Heathrow [hi:θ'rəʊ]
Hyde Park ['haɪd 'pɑ:k]
Jason ['dʒeɪsn]
Kashmir [kæʃ'mɪə]
Kensington ['kenzɪŋtn]
Kew Gardens ['kju: 'gɑ:dnz]
King's Cross ['kɪngz 'krɒs]
Leicester Square ['lestə 'skweə]
Little Venice ['lɪtl 'venɪs]
Lucy ['lu:sɪ]
Neil [ni:l]
New Cross ['nju: 'krɒs]
Paddington ['pædɪŋtn]
Patel [pə'tel]
Piccadilly Circus ['pɪkədɪlɪ 'sɜ:kəs]
Portobello Road ['pɔ:təbeləʊ 'rəʊd]
Queenswood ['kwi:nzwʊd]
Regent's Canal ['ri:dʒənts kə'næl]
Selfridges ['selfrɪdʒɪz]
Serpentine ['sɜ:pəntaɪn]
Thames [temz]
Tooting Bec ['tu:tɪŋ 'bek]
Tottenham Court Road ['tɒtnəm 'kɔ:t 'rəʊd]
Trafalgar Square [trə'fælgə 'skweə]
Victoria Station [vɪk'tɔ:rɪə 'steɪʃn]
Vincent ['vɪnsnt]
Westminster ['westmɪnstə]
Whitechapel ['waɪtʧæpl]

Fotoquellen

Adams Picture Library, London, S. 21 (links);
Barnabys Picture Library, London , S. 7, S. 17 (links), S. 19, S. 21 (rechts), S. 22;
The J. Allan Cash Photolibrary, London, S. 8, S. 12, S. 13, S. 14, S. 16, S. 26;
Sally & Richard Greenhill, London, S. 11;
Hunting Aerofilms, Boreham Wood, S. 4 (oben);
London Transport Museum, S. 4 (unten)
Museum of London, S. 17 (rechts);
Picturepoint, East Molesley, S. 9, S. 10, S. 15, S. 23;
Rick Wilson, London, S. 25.

Umschlagfoto

Picturepoint, East Molesley

Kartenmaterial

London Transport Museum, S. 40
Roy Schofield, Cheam, S. 38, S. 39

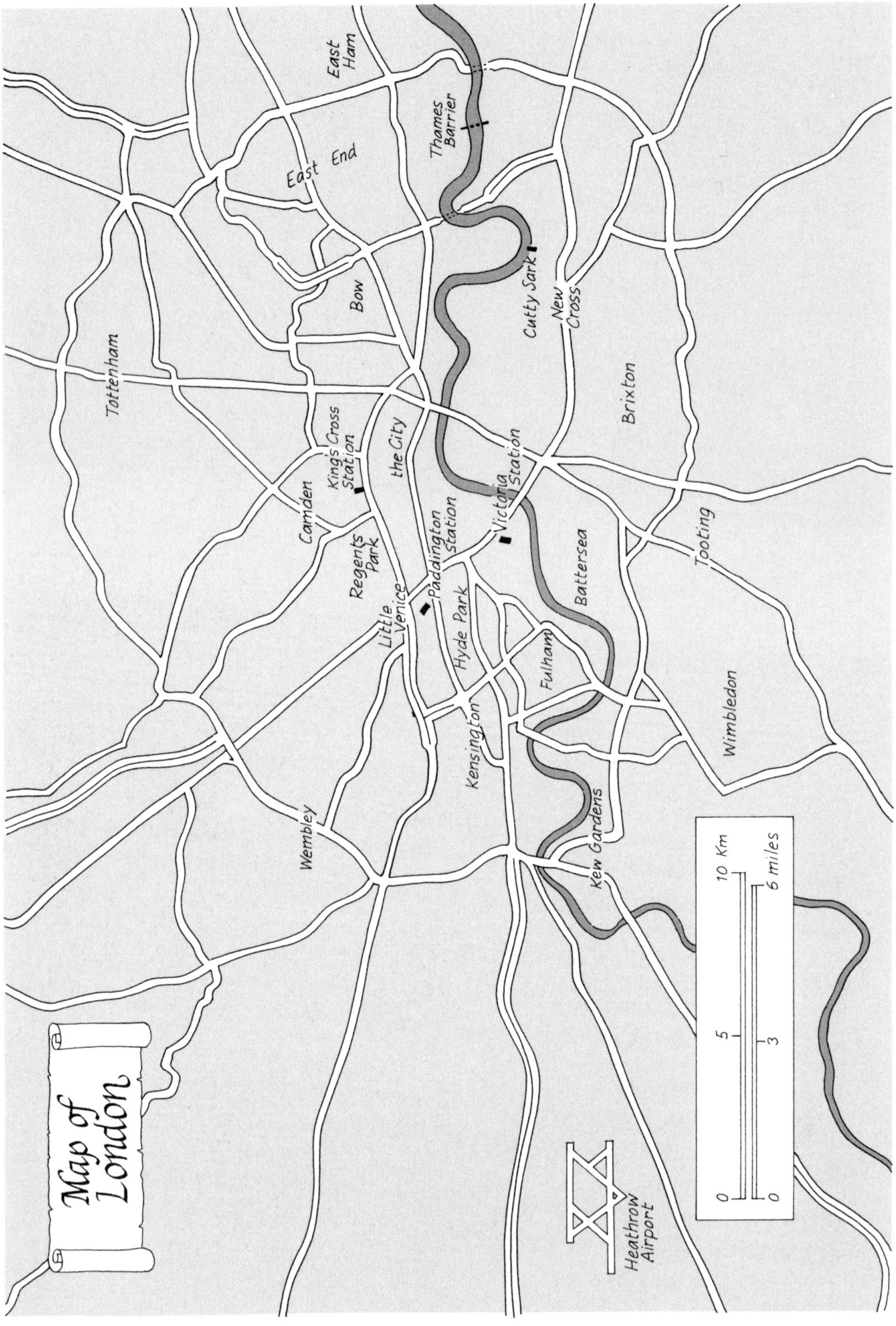
Map of London
East Ham
Thames Barrier
East End
Bow
Cutty Sark
New Cross
Tottenham
Brixton
Kings Cross Station
the City
Camden
Victoria Station
Paddington Station
Regents Park
Tooting
Battersea
Little Venice
Hyde Park
Fulham
Wimbledon
Kensington
Kew Gardens
Wembley
Heathrow Airport
0
5
10 Km
0
3
6 miles

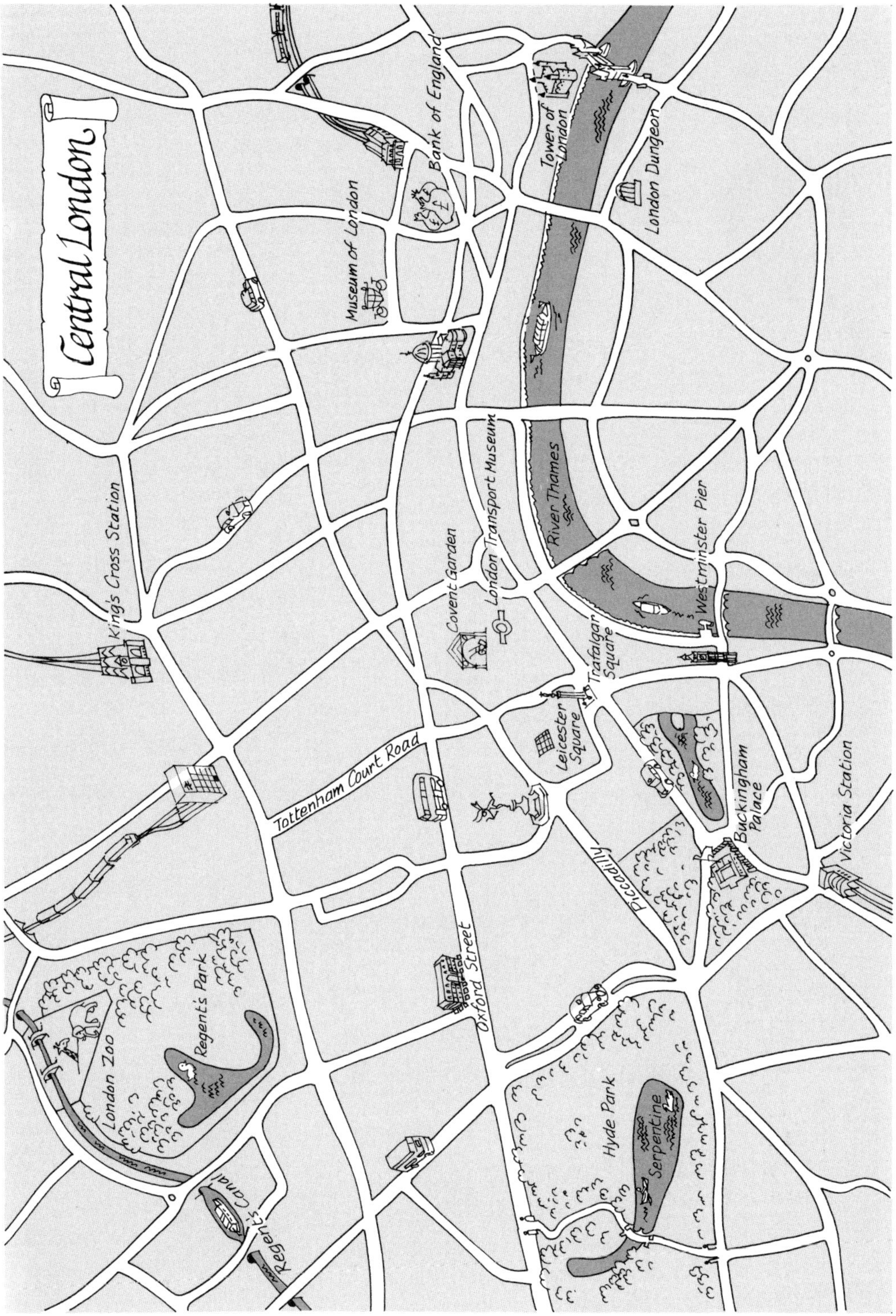
Central London
King's Cross Station
Museum of London
Bank of England
Tower of London
London Dungeon
River Thames
London Transport Museum
Covent Garden
Westminster Pier
Trafalgar Square
Leicester Square
Tottenham Court Road
Piccadilly
Buckingham Palace
Victoria Station
Oxford Street
Regent's Park
London Zoo
Regent's Canal
Hyde Park
Serpentine

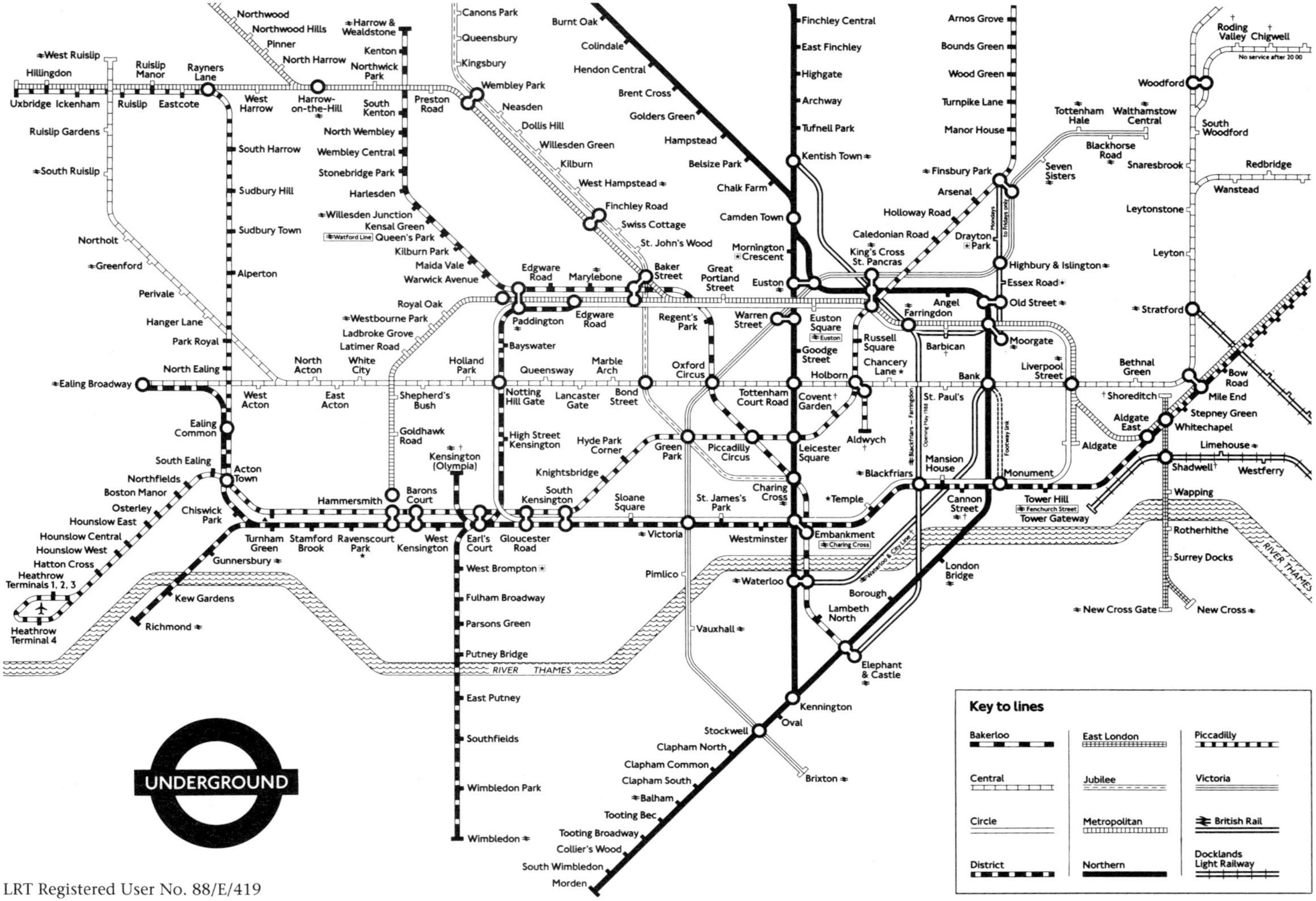

LRT Registered User No. 88/E/419